"I highly recommend the book The Abide Factor by Shawn Lyons. The practical wisdom he shares in this book will help you cultivate a harvest of God's blessings in all areas of your life. You just need to put it into practice. I appreciate the simple, down to earth way he explains how to abide in Christ. John 15 is one of my favorite chapters in the Bible, where Jesus states that a branch cannot be fruitful on its own, it must abide in the vine. Likewise, the only way for our lives to bear fruit is to abide or remain in Jesus. Apart from Him we can do nothing. By applying the principles outlined in this short book, your life will bear much fruit. Fruit that will last!"

Jeff Hill, Senior Pastor

New Hope Assembly of God - Urbandale, Iowa

"Shawn Lyons' The Abide Factor will bring much-needed clarity not only to what ABIDING IS but HOW to ABIDE in Christ! We all know that Abiding will bless us, that it is good for us - but many don't know HOW TO ABIDE! After reading The Abide Factor, you will be encouraged by the power of it while also being challenged to actually DO IT! John's second epistle says, 'those who do not abide in the teachings of Christ, do not have God' - so knowing how to ABIDE is extremely crucial for every believer!"

Jesse Newman, Lead Pastor

Eternity Church

THE
ABIDE FACTOR

A Biblically-based approach to living an abundant life and bearing fruit in Christ

SHAWN LYONS

Table of Contents

Foreword..i

Introduction From Broken to Whole...iii

Part One Abiding in Christ 1

Chapter One: A - Abide 5

Abide in Action: David... 10

Chapter Two: B - Bless 12

Abide in Action: A Restored Marriage 17

Chapter Three: I - Incline 18

Abide in Action: When Faith Multiplies 25

Chapter Four: D - Dwell 27

Abide in Action: The Author of Life................................. 30

Chapter Five: E - Everything 31

Part Two Bearing Fruit 33

Chapter Six: Spiritual Development.. 37

Chapter Seven: Character Development 38

Chapter Eight: Significant Relationships 39

Chapter Nine: Spending/Financial.. 40

Chapter Ten: Rhythm of Rest 42

Chapter Eleven: Daily Priority 43

Chapter Twelve: Physical 44

Conclusion and Next Steps.. 47

Afterword.. 49

About the Author 51

Foreword

I just finished reading one of the very best books in my life. "The Abide Factor" is a must read. It is a clear and concise teaching about how to truly abide in Christ and about the incredible blessings that happen as a result. While it is a short read it is packed with powerful truths that if applied will forever change you and your family. I've pastored for over 49 years and I've never read a better book. This book is a game changer. The end of the book breaks down step by step what it looks like to abide in Christ in every area of your life.

The stories in this book are true and so inspiring. One of the stories is written by Dave Grimm who is a dear friend of mine. I've personally seen his story happen before my eyes and I know it is largely because of his abiding faith in Jesus. He and Kelly and their four wonderful children are making a huge impact on the kingdom of God in central Iowa where they now live.

Buy several copies and give them to your family, friends and church members. It would be a great guide for a Bible study group as well.

James Weaver,

Founding Pastor of New Hope Assembly of God, Urbandale, Iowa

Introduction
From Broken to Whole

"I am the true vine, and My Father is the vinedresser. Every branch in Me that does not bear fruit He takes away; and every branch that bears fruit He prunes, that it may bear more fruit. You are already clean because of the word which I have spoken to you. Abide in Me, and I in you. As the branch cannot bear fruit of itself, unless it abides in the vine, neither can you, unless you abide in Me." - John 15:1-4

"Yet in all these things we are more than conquerors through Him who loved us. For I am persuaded that neither death nor life, nor angels nor principalities nor powers, nor things present nor things to come, nor height nor depth, nor any other created thing, shall be able to separate us from the love of God which is in Christ Jesus our Lord." - Romans 8:37-39

Let's start with a simple question - how are things working for you?

Perhaps your answer is positive. Maybe you feel good about where you are and where you're going. If so, that's great. I'm happy for you.

At the same time, I know that life is rarely (if ever) this simple. Chances are you feel unsatisfied or discontent with certain areas of your life. I've been in ministry for 37 years, and I've seen many people in this position. As Ecclesiastes 3:1 says, "To everything there is a season, A time for every purpose under heaven."

Perhaps you're hurting. Struggling. Feeling incapable of moving forward. Unsure of how to find your way. These are heavy burdens to carry, but hope remains.

It doesn't have to be this way. God created you for something better.

What I'm about to share with you isn't easy. It's a process that you'll have to be committed to, even on days when it isn't easy. However, I believe it's the road map to a better life. I've seen it work for hundreds (if not thousands) of people in the past, and you could be next.

It's a process that changed everything for me. And believe me, I desperately needed something to go my way.

When I was born, my stomach tube was closed. Before the surgery, I weighed only two pounds and four ounces. Even after the doctors resolved the issue with my stomach tube, I suffered from colic and cried often for months.

Things didn't improve much as I got older. I dealt with bad allergies and frequent ear infections, which led to hearing loss. I actually needed tubes inserted on multiple occasions because they wouldn't stay in my ears.

My parents chose to have me wait a year to start school because of my health issues. Most of my friends started first grade when they were six, but I didn't start until I turned seven.

This was when it seemed like everything around me was falling apart. After I finished first grade, my teacher called in my parents to tell them that something was wrong with me. They called me "dumb" and claimed that I couldn't learn like the other children.

Even though I was soon diagnosed with dyslexia, my teachers still had me sit in the corner with a "dunce" hat the following year in second grade. I was shamed and singled out as an eight-year-old child who had already been through so many struggles.

As if that wasn't bad enough, I had started to hear rumors that my mother didn't want me to be born. Before I came into the picture, my mother already had three children and had suffered two miscarriages. Turns out I was a mistake - and this was exactly how I felt.

The tipping point happened when I suffered abuse from a family member. I don't recall much about this time - or most other memories from my childhood before I turned 12 years old. Perhaps it's better this way.

What I do remember is that I felt broken. I couldn't comprehend any sort of future. That is, until I was saved by grace through faith in Jesus. For the first time in my life, I felt loved and accepted. As a 12-year-old boy – even after all that I had gone through – I felt a call to preach God's Word. I'm still amazed that God would choose to take someone like me and use me for His glory.

Paul writes in Galatians 2:20, "I have been crucified with Christ; it is no longer I who live, but Christ lives in me." He also writes in Philippians 4 that we can do all things through Christ who strengthens us (Phil. 4:13). These teachings are incredibly freeing and exciting for me. When I come to the end of my own ability or capability, I can rely on the power and presence of Jesus in my life.

I'll never forget the powerful reality that hit me one day as I was reading John 15. On the night before He goes to the cross, Jesus calls His disciples to abide in Him. He tells them that as a branch can't bear fruit on its own, they cannot do anything apart from the Father.

This teaching literally changed my life. It set me free from all the pain and brokenness I experienced earlier in life. I had already seen what life was like without God's presence, and I knew that I couldn't do anything apart from Him. But what was truly exciting was imagining what was possible in my life if I remained connected to the Vine.

Abide is a primary verb. It means to stay, to continue, to dwell, to be present, or to remain. After I read John 15 for the first time, I desperately wanted to abide in Christ. However, I knew it would require a pivot in my life. I knew that I would need to keep my focus on Jesus at all times. I understood that what I fed would grow, and what I starved would die.

If I wanted to abide in Jesus, I had to let go of all the pain and rejection from my past. I would have to follow the example set by Paul in Philippians 3 when he says, "Forgetting those things which are behind and reaching forward to those things which are ahead, I press toward the goal for the prize of the upward call of God in Christ Jesus." (Phil. 3:13-14) I imagined the journey wouldn't always be easy, but I knew it would be worth it.

I believe this same transformation is possible for each person reading this book. It doesn't matter what you've experienced in the past. It doesn't matter where you're starting from. It doesn't matter how much wealth, power, or influence you have. If you approach God with open hands and an open heart, ready for whatever direction He chooses to lead you in, you can have a life that is rich and abundant with God's blessings.

Our hope is that this book gives you a glimpse into how you can live this type of blessed life. We'll start by introducing you to The Abide Factor. Based on Jesus' words to His disciples in John 15, we believe that The Abide Factor is the secret to living a life of faithfulness and obedience to Christ.

In the following section, we'll cover seven practical steps to put The Abide Factor into practice in a way that produces fruit in your daily life. Before we wrap up, we'll tell you about our mentorship program where you can partner with an experienced guide who will help you apply all the concepts you read about in this book. For more information about mentorship, visit our website at www.provenresultsmentors.com.

Ready to get started? Great. Let's take a deeper look at what it really means to "abide."

Part One
Abiding in Christ

Why are you here? What's brought you to this moment? Why do you feel the way that you do now?

Like the map in a shopping mall or an airport terminal marked with a "You are Here" stamp to tell you where you currently stand, you must understand where you are before you can determine where you're going.

At the same time, no matter where you find your stamp on the map, you have control over where you go next. Once you know where you are, you have full control over your next steps. You have the freedom to imagine what your future could look like. Once you decide on the destination, you can work backward to create the steps between where you are and where you want to go.

This is incredibly powerful because without a compelling vision for the future, you'll never fulfill your potential or create the kind of life you truly want to live. A person can have great intentions but still struggle to move forward because they don't proactively design their days and prime their environment around what matters most to them. Remember that what you feed grows, and what you starve dies. You'll always be trapped if you dwell on your fear, pain, hurt, or frustration.

So the first step to changing your position in life requires changing your focus. That's what The ABIDE Factor is all about. We've created a framework that empowers people, regardless of their past experiences or present circumstances, to break free from the struggles and limitations that hold them back. We cannot wait to share The ABIDE Factor with you in the chapters ahead.

Inside The ABIDE Factor are five words, each one containing a powerful truth about how God created each of us and the world we live in:

- **A - Abide.** We turn our attention to Jesus by looking to Him as our source and guide.
- **B - Bless.** We bless God through obeying His Word and keeping His commandments.
- **I - Incline.** We listen to God's Word and turn our hearts toward His values and principles. We train ourselves to hear God's voice and respond when He calls.
- **D - Dwell.** We stay close to God by remaining mindful of His presence in our daily lives.
- **E - Everything.** As Jesus commands us in Matthew 22:37-38, we love God with everything we have.

The ABIDE Factor reminds us that we reap what we sow. If we work hard to develop good habits, cultivate strong values, and participate in the work that God has called us to, we will reap a harvest beyond our wildest dreams. This opportunity is available for all who hear God's calling. It's now up to you how you will respond.

Before we go forward, you must make a commitment to yourself. Decide right now that you're going to change your focus. From this moment on, your life is no longer about the things that defeat you or hold you back from reaching your potential. It's time to pivot. It's time to put all of our attention into the things that bring us life and help us thrive. There's an entirely new realm of possibility and growth that lies ahead. Ready to see it for yourself? Great. Let your journey begin!

Chapter One: A - Abide

"She won't survive the next two hours. You should get ready to go in and say goodbye."

As I sat in the waiting room of the trauma department with a couple from my church, I was saddened to hear the doctor's bleak prognosis. Their daughter had been in a horrific car accident. She suffered from multiple broken bones and numerous cuts and bruises. Her lungs were collapsed, and she was headed for organ failure as a result of intense trauma.

As I watched her parents process the news, I was shocked by the mother's response. To be honest, I hadn't seen this level of faith at any prior point in my ministry.

Even while coming to terms with the possibility of losing her daughter, she reaffirmed her faith in Jesus. She reflected on the moment shortly after her daughter's birth when they brought her to the altar at church and dedicated her life to God. She proclaimed that they would continue to trust God no matter what happened to their daughter.

Something began to stir inside of me. I reached out my hands and asked the girl's father to place his hands on mine. While it may seem like a strange request, it's what I felt the Holy Spirit leading me to do.

My hands began to burn. The girl's father immediately noticed the heat when I touched his hands. I instructed him to go into the hospital room and lay hands on his daughter. Even though his hands were shaking by this point, he went into the room and did as I instructed. Little did they know a miracle was about to take place.

I remain amazed by this couple's faith to this day. In spite of everything happening to them at the moment, they chose to hang onto their faith in God. They never wavered or doubted despite the challenges they were facing. In their darkest hour, they learned what it truly meant to abide.

When the girl survived past the next two hours, the doctor's prognosis didn't change. He cautioned her parents against building false hope and still felt as though the injuries would be too great to overcome.

Seventeen years later, the girl is married with three children and a successful career. We serve a God who is capable of the impossible.

What might God choose to do in your life if you make the decision to abide in Him?

Among the four Gospel accounts in the New Testament, the Gospel of John is unique. Unlike Matthew, Mark, and Luke (which most scholars call the "synoptic" Gospels), the Gospel of John takes a different approach to telling the story of Jesus' life and teachings.

In the Gospel of John, we get an inside view of a scene from Jesus' life that occurred the night before His crucifixion. Jesus spends the evening celebrating Passover with His disciples in an intimate setting. The evening begins with Jesus washing His disciples' feet - a striking visual of service and self-sacrifice that would have knocked the disciples' socks off (pun intended).

After this, Jesus breaks bread with His disciples and begins to teach them. This was not uncommon - by this point, the disciples had heard Jesus teach about many subjects on various occasions. However, something was different in this setting. The disciples could sense that everything was about to change, but nothing Jesus said could fully prepare them for what was ahead.

One of Jesus' key messages from His speech the night before his death, which some bible scholars call the Farewell Discourse, has to do with the importance of abiding. After Jesus foretells the coming of the Holy Spirit, He encourages His disciples to abide in Himself. Take a look at Jesus' words from John 15:4-7.

"Abide in Me, and I in you. As the branch cannot bear fruit of itself, unless it abides in the vine, neither can you, unless you abide in Me. I am the vine, you are the branches. He who abides in Me, and I in him, bears much fruit; for without Me you can do nothing. If anyone does not abide in Me, he is cast out as a branch and is withered; and they gather them and throw them into the fire, and they are burned. If you abide in Me, and My words abide in you, you will ask what you desire, and it shall be done for you."

The word "abide" jumps off the page for today's readers and would have rung loudly in the disciples' ears when they heard Jesus use it repeatedly. But what exactly does this word mean? Our English word "abide" is an active verb that means to tolerate a difficult situation, withstand the threat of potential obstacles, or accept a verdict or decision without opposition. In the original Greek, Jesus used the word "meinate," which often translates to "abide" or "remain." Jesus used the same word in Matthew 26:38 and Mark 14:34 when He asked the disciples to remain with Him in the Garden of Gethsemane when He prayed on the night before His betrayal.

In both situations, the challenge is the same. Abiding in Jesus requires staying when it would be easier to go. Although the disciples didn't know what challenges were awaiting them when Jesus encouraged them to "abide in Him" before His betrayal, it didn't take long before they presented themselves. Tradition holds that all of Jesus' closest disciples died as martyrs because of their faith. John was the lone exception – his life ended in exile after an unsuccessful attempt by the Romans to take his life. According to the early Christian author Tertullian, the Romans submerged John in boiling oil, but he was unharmed.

Many modern-day American Christians don't have to worry about being put to death for their faith, but this doesn't mean that following God is (or should be) easy. Jesus is the living embodiment of sacrifice, and as His followers, we shouldn't expect anything less in our own lives. This means that if we're going to abide, we have to transform our minds. We must be willing to make a change. We have to pivot.

This starts by looking to Jesus as our source of all provision and blessings in life. Remember, what you feed will grow, and what you starve will die. If you commit to filling your mind with the teachings and promises of Jesus, your faith will grow, and you'll be better equipped to respond to the challenges of life. If you focus instead on your fears and insecurities (or even selfish ambitions), you'll set yourself up to fail.

Once again, this doesn't mean that life will always be easy. Thankfully, we can find courage and motivation in Jesus' example. As Hebrews 12:2 reminds us, Jesus endured the cross "for the joy that was set before him." In the process, He "(despised) the shame" and "set down at the right hand of the throne of God."

When you choose to abide in Christ, you find the solution to the internal tension that we all feel. Each person wants to find purpose and meaning in life. Many people try to fill it with money, power, influence, or success. Like the well that the Samaritan woman draws from in John 4, each ultimately leaves us feeling empty and needing to return to the well for another drink.

The presence of God is different. In Jesus, we find the living water that is eternally satisfying. He wants to offer you the love, joy, peace, and happiness you've been searching for. Once you experience a new life in Jesus, you'll no longer feel an internal ache. Instead, you'll experience a newfound sense of contentment as you live each day in His new life.

Before we wrap up, here's one practical step to help you get started. **Take time each day to focus on your relationship with God.** It doesn't have to be the same time every day, but it's important to eliminate distractions so that you can properly focus and dedicate a few minutes to the Lord. Maybe you take a moment to pray each time you find yourself in a challenging situation. Perhaps you decide to set aside a few moments each morning to read a chapter or two in your Bible. I know many people who benefit greatly from setting aside 10-15 minutes daily to pray. What makes this time special is that they don't spend the entire time talking - they also spend a few moments listening to what God has to say to them.

The specific activity doesn't matter as much as the discipline to practice this habit consistently. If you prioritize your relationship with God, everything else will come into alignment. Abide in the Father, and He will bear fruit in your life.

Abide in Action: David

My name is David. I live in Iowa with my wife and our four children.

We have been business owners for almost 11 years. For seven of those 11 years, we've been working on growing a Chick-fil-A franchise in West Des Moines. We've seen tremendous growth, and we're now running the busiest Chick-fil-A in the state.

Most recently, we've been operating one of only 31 Chick-fil-A food trucks in the nation. We love Chick-fil-A so much that we want people across Iowa to have the opportunity to try our food.

Of course, the journey into business wasn't & isn't easy. I spent twelve years in ministry before making the decision to open a restaurant. One year after we opened our first Mexican restaurant in a mall in Monroeville, PA, we witnessed a mall shooting. Not long after, a riot involving over 100 teenagers also happened at our mall. Suddenly, nobody wanted to come to our mall, and our sales started to plummet.

My wife and I had four children under four years old at the time, and I was quickly growing desperate. I was eight months behind on rent, and we were relying on supplier food credits to prevent us from getting behind on our bills.

One night, I didn't have enough gas money to get home. As I walked toward the freight elevator, I thought about Pastor Shawn's lesson from the previous Sunday. He told the story of Jesus instructing Peter to catch a fish & then pull a coin out of its mouth to pay their taxes.

I prayed that prayer before stepping on the freight elevator. To my surprise, I found a $10 bill inside the elevator. It was the exact amount of money I needed to make the 45-minute trip home, and get back to work the next day.

I appreciated the blessing, but I still had problems. We didn't have enough to pay our bills and purchase groceries. What should I do?

I didn't have to make that decision because God stepped in. He spoke to the heart of a woman in our church who purchased three months' worth of groceries for us. She even found the specific formula my youngest daughter needed because of her dairy intolerance. God must have told her what we needed, because we hadn't shared this with anybody else.

Sadly, my mom passed away from breast cancer during this season in our lives. Her employer sponsored a fundraiser to promote breast cancer research. Once they reached their goal, they gave the rest of the money to her children. The timing couldn't have been better for us. The sewage pump in our home was broken, and we were brushing our teeth outside in the middle of the snow because we couldn't afford to fix it.

Moments like these made me wonder what I was doing with my life. However, I saw God respond to my needs time and time again. These trials reminded me that God was my sole provider and that He could deliver me through any circumstance.

Fast forward to today. Our Chick-fil-A is expected to exceed $13 million in sales this year. We've given away hundreds of thousands of dollars in tuition assistance and food donations. We've seen over 100 employees choose to give their lives to Christ. We believe we're still doing ministry, just in an occupational sense (I call it fried chicken evangelism).

If I've learned anything in my life, it's that God can do amazing things when we align our hearts with His Word. When you make the decision to abide in Christ, you'll be amazed at what God has in store for you!

Chapter Two: B - Bless

Do you ever feel like you aren't good enough? Does it seem like you don't deserve God's love or mercy? Do you wonder how you could ever measure up to others' expectations?

I know I've been there. Because of the way that I grew up, I had plenty of hurdles to overcome. It's an understatement to say that life didn't always go the way I thought it would (or the way I wanted).

Thankfully, after I came to faith in Jesus, my understanding began to shift. I realized that I could find peace and strength in the Lord even when life didn't go the way I wanted. I realized that peace was found in Jesus and not in the absence of problems or trials. This recognition made me want to bless the Lord in all that I did.

If I had to point to a single verse that shifted my perspective on the importance of blessing God, I would probably choose Colossians 3:17: "And whatever you do, in word or deed, do everything in the name of the Lord Jesus, giving thanks to God the Father through him."

I spent years wrestling with feelings of inadequacy before I found Jesus. Once I realized that in Jesus I had all I needed, I decided to go all in. I spent as much time as I could with my church family. At one point, I was going four times each week. I went to youth group meetings on Tuesday and Thursday evenings in addition to all-church services on Sunday morning and Sunday night.

I almost turned down a job because it would impact my ability to be with my youth group on Tuesday and Thursday nights. I was interviewing for a job at a local family-owned Italian restaurant when I was 15. During the interview, the owner said that he would need me to work Monday through Saturday. I told him I would love the job, but I couldn't work on Tuesdays or Thursdays. The owner asked why I wasn't available those nights, so I told him about my youth group. To my surprise, the owner was impressed by my dedication to my faith and told me that he thought I was someone he could depend on because of my commitment to my church.

Even if the owner wasn't willing to be flexible with my hours, I still wouldn't have changed my mind about my weekly youth group meetings. I knew what was most important to me, and I wasn't willing to negotiate. After all, how could I not put God first after all He had done for me? I was committed to abiding in Him and blessing him with my life.

I deeply appreciate the words of the Psalmist in Psalm 18:

> I will bless the Lord at all times: his praise shall continually be in my mouth.

> My soul shall make her boast in the Lord: the humble shall hear thereof, and be glad.

> O magnify the Lord with me, and let us exalt his name together.

> I sought the Lord, and he heard me, and delivered me from all my fears.

> They looked unto him, and were lightened: and their faces were not ashamed.

> This poor man cried, and the Lord heard him, and saved him out of all his troubles.

> The angel of the Lord encampeth round about them that fear him, and delivereth them.

> O taste and see that the Lord is good: blessed is the man that trusteth in him.

Even after many years, these words continue to blow me away. How could anyone *not* want to bless God after reading this passage?

To bless God is to serve others in His name. To bless God is to abide in His Word, knowing that it will produce life-altering transformation in our hearts and minds. To bless God is to understand the potential impact of this transformation – not only in our lives but in the lives of the people around us.

This all begins with the understanding that none of this is possible unless we abide in Christ. As Jesus reminds His disciples in John 15, nothing is possible apart from Him: "As the branch cannot bear fruit of itself, unless it abides in the vine, neither can you, unless you abide in me."

It's hard to underestimate the impact of the word "unless" in this passage. In many ways, this verse presents a theme dominant throughout the New Testament and through our Christian faith. Without the two phrases that begin with "unless," this sentence takes on a very different meaning.

Imagine how the verse would read if you eliminated the two "unless" phrases. "As the branch cannot bear fruit of itself, neither can you." That's it. Full stop. It's a closed door with no hope. Without Christ in our lives, we have no potential. We don't bring anything to the table.

Everything changes when the word "unless" comes into the picture. "As the branch cannot bear fruit of itself, unless it abides in the vine, neither can you, unless you abide in me." Because God the Father Himself came to earth in the person of Jesus Christ, we have an unlimited power source to tap into that can quite literally change the world. And it all starts with us, as followers of Jesus, making a choice to abide in Him.

Once we make the decision to abide in Christ, this mindset must become practical through our actions. I can't help but think about the words of James in his letter written to exiles in the early days of the church:

> "What does it profit, my brethren, if someone says he has faith but does not have works? Can faith save him? If a

brother or sister is naked and destitute of daily food, and one of you says to them, "Depart in peace, be warmed and filled," but you do not give them the things which are needed for the body, what does it profit? Thus also faith by itself, if it does not have works, is dead." - James 2:14-16

James' point is not that our works save us. We're incapable of earning our salvation - this is only possible through the grace of God displayed in Jesus' death on the cross. However, when we make Jesus the Lord of our lives, the only natural response is to allow faith to display itself in our actions.

Imagine you're trapped inside a burning building. Thankfully, you know that there's a safe way out that will allow you to escape unharmed. If you truly believe that the building is in danger, what would you do? Would you stay inside and hope for the best, or would you make your way toward the exit as quickly as possible?

The same principle is true here. If you really believe that Jesus was God in the flesh, and that He was crucified for the sins of the world and resurrected in three days, you must do something. This isn't just a fun fact or an interesting tidbit. It's a life-altering truth.

Obeying the commandments of Jesus begins with knowing His teachings. Once we understand the kind of life that Jesus calls us to live, we begin to put these principles into action. We'll never be perfect (and that's a good reminder of the grace that we all need), but we must always strive to grow in our faith and better embody the heart and mind of Jesus.

Shortly before introducing the concept of abiding, Jesus reminds His disciples of the importance of keeping the Father's commandments. In John 14:23-24, Jesus says, "If anyone loves Me, he will keep My word; and My Father will love him, and we will come to him and make Our home with him. He who does not love Me does not keep My words; and the word which you hear is not Mine but the Father's who sent Me."

Something powerful happens when we begin to put these teachings into practice. When we bless Jesus through service and obedience (and reinforce that connection between ourselves and the Father), God begins to work in our lives. You'll notice a difference in your thoughts, actions, and relationships as you begin to pursue righteousness and holiness in all you do. As Jesus teaches us in the Sermon on the Mount, we will receive when we ask and we will find when we seek (Matthew 7:7).

If you're in a difficult situation right now, I hope this offers you a sense of hope. Even when you don't see it, God is still near. God can breathe life into the worst of circumstances. God can draw near even when everything around you is falling apart. If you're already living in abundance, God can make a good situation even better. You may even find that your desires come into greater alignment with God's plans and purposes for the world as you pursue Godliness in a more consistent manner.

Before we wrap up, let's think about how this looks in a practical manner. Today, I encourage you to take one concrete step to bless God. Each day, we run across numerous opportunities to put our faith into action. We often miss these chances because we're too distracted by other pursuits. Let today be the first day when you take a different approach. Commit to being mindful of the needs that exist around you, and look for opportunities to be the hands and feet of Jesus in a practical way.

Here are a few ideas or examples to get you started:

1. Encourage a friend by telling them that you love them and you want to help them however you can.
2. Pray for someone in your life who has a need, and look for practical ways to step in and fill that need.
3. Find a way to serve someone near you who is incapable of helping themselves. Maybe you have an elderly neighbor who struggles to get around. What if you could mow their lawn or bring their garbage cans down to the curb?
4. If you have extra financial resources, consider paying for someone's groceries or extending a gift to someone who is having difficulty making ends meet.

Abide in Action: A Restored Marriage

Their relationship had reached a breaking point. Unless something changed, divorce seemed inevitable.

I remember the night I received that phone call. On the other end, I heard a strong sense of desperation and urgency. Years of being in a toxic relationship were beginning to take their toll, and something needed to be different.

We set an appointment for the following day. I hoped I could help this couple get to the root of their issues. I knew that if Jesus could enter the picture, it wouldn't take long for healing and reconciliation to take place.

For the next six weeks, I sat down with this couple once per week. We went through each step of The Abide Factor in detail. As this couple learned what it meant to abide in Christ, they began to leave behind their disappointment and hurt. They replaced unhealthy practices with a life-giving relationship with Jesus. For the first time, they experienced true healing, forgiveness, and transformation.

Although they regretted the years they had wasted, they were grateful for the healing and restoration they experienced through the power of Christ. They looked forward to applying their new wisdom and understanding, and they knew that it would strengthen and bless their marriage for years to come.

Chapter Three: I - Incline

The commitment to abide in the Lord is a commitment to a better way. To commit to following God's commandments is to commit to obedience. And this obedience starts by inclining our hearts to God's Word and trusting in His ability to guide our lives.

I remember a time in my life when I learned a great deal about the importance of trusting God's provision. I was newly married and working a full-time job while studying to enter the ministry. One day, I woke up and found out that the department I was working in would soon close down. By this point, we had a house, a new car, and a baby on the way. Not an ideal situation for a 22-year-old and his 18-year-old wife.

We pulled up to church. My wife said, "Shawn, we have very little food at home, and we're down to a quarter tank of gas. The only money we have left is our small tithe. What should we do?"

It was a moment that I'll never forget. We had a decision to make. We could be faithful to the Lord, or we could keep the money for ourselves (effectively taking the matter of provision into our own hands).

We had major needs, but we believed that God was bigger than our situation. We decided to return to the Lord the money that was already His. That day, when service ended, a man walked up to me and shook my hand. There was a piece of paper in his hand that I later found out was a check. I hadn't told anyone besides God about my family's needs, but the man told me to take the check.

Soon after, I went to hug another man, and he put his hand in my pocket. I was terrified. I thought he was about to take the money. I'm not sure if he noticed the horrified look on my face or not, but he told me that he felt God leading him to bless me today.

We felt God bless us in a major way that day in response to our decision to obey His instructions. All of a sudden, we had more than enough to get us through the entire month. Nearly 38 years have passed since this day, and we haven't doubted God's provision once.

In that moment (and in many others), I learned about the importance of obeying God's instructions. In John 15, Jesus shares the following words with His disciples: "If ye keep my commandments, ye shall abide in my love; even as I have kept my Father's commandments, and abide in his love." I consider this Scripture to be a non-negotiable commitment to God's way, which is a far better way than anything I could come up with on my own.

Through the years, we've had the pleasure of serving full-time with four different churches. We've been with our current congregation for almost 24 years. Before we came here, we were on staff with an amazing church close to a large city. The congregation had around 450 members, and I served as the associate pastor and the youth pastor.

One day while serving with that congregation, I attended a funeral for a family friend. The funeral procession took us through a scenic countryside route on the way to the cemetery. As I drove, I noticed a church in the middle of a cornfield. I remember thinking to myself, who would want to attend a church like that one in the middle of nowhere?

Looking back, I realize that God must have a sense of humor. More importantly, His plans are far greater than anything our own minds could come up with.

About a year later, I was invited to speak at a church that was searching for a new pastor. At the time, the church had employed five different pastors in six years. I didn't realize it at the time when I accepted the invitation, but I had agreed to travel and speak at the same cornfield church in the middle of nowhere.

When we pulled into the parking lot, my wife asked me a question. The situation wasn't dissimilar from several years earlier when we were faced with the decision to hold onto our tithe or be faithful to God's calling. Once again, I sat in the car with my wife in the parking lot before church and had to contemplate a major decision.

"Shawn, we're moving here, aren't we?"

I thought for a moment, but it was obvious what direction I should take.

"Yes, it looks like we are," I responded.

Twenty-four years later, I'll still admit that I never saw myself pastoring in this type of situation. However, we chose to be obedient to God's plan. On our first Sunday, there were around 35 people in attendance. Today, our membership is closer to 250. I guess I underestimated the appeal of a church in a cornfield in the middle of nowhere.

We've faced our fair share of challenges over the years, but we serve a God far bigger than the opposition. Our church is incredibly loving and welcoming – full of people who understand they are called by God to do great things. Two years before we came to town, it was prophesied that God would pour out His Spirit in this area, and great things would happen. The prophet predicted that God would reach people in all four corners of the world because of the work that has happened in this church.

Fast forward to today. Our sermons have been downloaded in 48 of the 50 US states and in over 95 different countries. We average around 20,000 downloads a year. In addition, we have built five churches and a parsonage in southern Mexico in the past three decades. We've partnered with various efforts in India to teach women to sew and to build an orphanage. We have also supported work in Russia, Africa, and in the Czech Republic.

At the same time, we are just as concerned with helping our neighbors as we are with serving people on the other side of the globe. Our back-to-school outreach has taken place each year for the past 20 plus years. We've given away over 20,000 backpacks filled with school supplies. We've provided haircuts to over 3,000 children and adults, and we have fed over 20,000 people. Each day, our daycare center provides care for over 120 local children. Not bad for a church in the middle of nowhere!

Just to clarify, I'm not taking credit for any of this. This is God's story, not mine. These examples serve as a powerful reminder that all things are possible with God. I'm continually amazed at God's ability to use a group of humble people to bring great honor and glory to Himself.

I believe the same thing is possible for you. God is ready, willing, and able to do something powerful in your life when you make the decision to respond to Him in obedience.

There's an old hymn written by John H. Sammis called "Trust and Obey." Perhaps you've heard the familiar refrain: "Trust and obey, for there's no other way to be happy in Jesus but to trust and obey." When I look back on my life, the decision to trust and obey has made an immensely profound impact that I'm eternally grateful for. Could the same be possible for you?

Once you make the decision to abide in Christ and bless God through your actions, something starts to change inside of you. You begin to see the world from a Godly perspective. You start to care more for others than you do for yourself. You find yourself responding differently to adversity, fear, or uncertainty. You experience joy from new sources.

This is an incredible feeling, and it's evidence of transformation only possible through the Holy Spirit. In 2 Corinthians 5:17, Paul writes, "Therefore, if anyone is in Christ, he is a new creation; old things have passed away; behold, all things have become new." When you begin to experience this new birth in Christ, you experience what it feels like to naturally incline your heart towards God and His Word.

As a verb, "incline" has multiple definitions. The first is to feel willingly or favorably disposed toward a particular feeling, action, or decision. The second definition is to have a particular tendency. In either scenario, it suggests a feeling of intuition or predisposition that makes a certain type of response easier. It reflects an innate feeling or motivation that comes naturally.

In some cases, our inclinations are tendencies that we're born with. Other times, we learn them through experience. What's important to note here is that we don't have to be controlled by our negative inclinations. We can reverse these trends. We can rewire our minds.

At the same time, if you have an inclination that helps you, you should continue to let it work in your favor. If you're inclined to choose a salad when a cheeseburger is also an option, give me a call. I'd love to learn from you.

So what does this have to do with abiding in Christ? We can train ourselves to incline our hearts and minds to God's Word in a manner that helps us put His teachings and examples into action. At first, this will require a great degree of effort and intentionality. Over time, it will become natural and habitual.

Once again, James provides a great reminder of what this concept looks like in action. In James 1, he writes about a man who hears God's teaching but doesn't act on what he has learned:

> "But be doers of the word, and not hearers only, deceiving yourselves. For if anyone is a hearer of the word and not a doer, he is like a man observing his natural face in a mirror; for he observes himself, goes away, and immediately forgets what kind of man he was. But he who looks into the perfect law of liberty and continues *in it,* and is not a forgetful hearer but a doer of the work, this one will be blessed in what he does." - James 1:22-25

In other words, the first step of inclining toward God is hearing what He has to say to us in His Word. However, this isn't the only step. We must also take what we hear and put it into practice. For you, this could mean taking notes on Scripture as you read. For someone else, the best way to internalize God's teaching may be to memorize portions of Scripture and reflect on them throughout the day. Practicing habits like these will enable God's truth to take root in your heart and be the guiding force behind all of your thoughts and actions.

We live in a world where we are constantly receiving messages. Whether it's through an email from a coworker, an advertisement on social media, or a text from a friend, the average person hears between 20,000 and 30,000 words each day. It's easy to hold God's Word in the same regard as all of these other words because of the manner in which we are overwhelmed with content on a daily basis.

If we're going to avoid the temptation to become desensitized to the life-changing, inspiring, world-shaking truth contained in God's Word, we must allow space for God's Word to take root in our hearts and work in our lives. Imagine how your life could be different if you set aside time each day to study God's Word and let it impact the way you live your life. What might God want to do in you?

The story of Peter in Matthew 14 is a great example of what can happen when you take the Word of God seriously and incline your mind to obey God's truth. Peter is on a boat with the rest of the disciples when they see Jesus coming toward them on the water. Like the other disciples, Peter is initially startled. Once he realizes that he's seeing Jesus and not a ghost, he asks Jesus to call to him. Jesus invites Peter to come to Him on the water, and that's exactly what Peter does…for a few moments. Soon after Peter begins walking on water, fear settles back in, and he begins to sink.

It's easy to focus on the fact that Peter lost faith. However, let us not ignore the fact that for a short time, Peter was doing the impossible. He walked on water! This was only possible because he inclined himself to the calling of Jesus. Jesus invites Peter to walk on water, and that's what Peter does – even if only for a short time.

Like Peter, Jesus is calling you. He's called you to do more, to be more, to live for more. Jesus' calling requires faith, but as we've already learned, there's tremendous possibility and power available to anyone who chooses to abide in the Lord. What will you experience when you make the decision to abide in Christ, bless God through service, and incline your heart to His Word?

To prepare yourself to respond to this calling, speak out loud the words from Psalm 119:105 to yourself: "Your word is a lamp to my feet And a light to my path." Next, consider how God may prompt you to act today. As we covered in the previous chapter, God gives us opportunities each day to respond in faith and obedience. However, we often miss out on chances to put our faith in action because we are busy, distracted, or simply disinterested.

Today can be different, but only if you make the intentional decision to open your eyes to the brokenness and injustice in the world around you. How will you respond to God today? How will you give your time and resources in a way that serves others? How will you help those who can't help themselves? How will you encourage someone who is hurting or struggling?

Incline yourself to respond to God. You'll be amazed at what happens next.

Abide in Action: When Faith Multiplies

In each of the Gospel accounts, we read a story of Jesus feeding a large crowd with the amount of food you would expect to find inside a Lunchable. If you aren't familiar with the feeding of the 5,000, Jesus takes a small basket containing five loaves of bread and two fish. He blesses the food and instructs His disciples to begin distributing the meal. Jesus multiples the food and provides enough for 5,000 men to eat. After everyone has enough to eat, there are still twelve baskets full of leftover food.

God is still in the business of multiplication. I once knew a young family tasked with taking over their family business. They were facing many challenges and felt uncertain about the future.

One Sunday morning during our church's worship service, I felt called to invite this family to the altar so our church could pray over them. As our leaders prayed for them, I sensed the Holy Spirit giving me specific instructions to share with them. I challenged them to be faithful to what God was directing them to do. If they were obedient, God would add to their business.

When they received the first instruction, they responded in faith. Not long after, their business doubled. As remarkable as that is, God wasn't finished. He gave them another instruction, and once again, they responded in faith and their business multiplied.

While we were excited to see their business grow, we were even more grateful for the lesson they learned about abiding in Christ and being faithful stewards of the blessings they received from God. This young family learned to hear God's voice and respond in obedience. As they made these choices, God made His presence known in their lives and provided us all with a practical reminder of how He draws near to those who are faithful to His Word.

Chapter Four: D - Dwell

"There is a time for everything, and a season for every activity under the heavens."

Ecclesiastes 3:1

We live in a world where people are constantly on the move. It seems like the grass is always greener in another job or in a different relationship. It's easy to forget about the power of staying in a situation (even if it's not perfect) and reaping the benefits that God chooses to offer those who commit to long-term faithfulness.

I've been in my current pastoral position for over 24 years. Over the years, I've had a few opportunities to leave to serve with another church. On the surface, they all seemed like great opportunities. The churches were growing and they had more resources.

At first glance, things seemed perfect – especially when I had the opportunity to move to Florida. After all, I had suffered through Pennsylvania winters for nearly sixty years. Perhaps this was God's reward for my perseverance!

However, I couldn't shake the sense that it wasn't God's plan for us. I felt then (and still do) that God wants me to remain where I am, so I choose to stay. Throughout my life, I've chosen to stay faithful to God's calling and direction for my life. I find peace in the knowledge that I'm wherever God wants me to be.

As I contemplate the idea of remaining in one place, my mind goes back to John 15. In Verse 9, Jesus encourages His disciples to continue (or remain) in His love. There's tremendous power in learning to remain in God's love (and in whatever situation He has you in). God has major plans in store for those who choose to dwell in His love.

27

Love is God's defining aspect. If you read Scripture, you'll learn about all facets of God. You'll gain exposure to God's justice, mercy, provision, wrath, and judgment. At the end of the day, each of these aspects on their own fail to fully describe God's heart or personality. Where they fall short, love succeeds.

Think about this passage from 1 John: " Beloved, let us love one another, for love is of God; and everyone who loves is born of God and knows God. He who does not love does not know God, for God is love. In this the love of God was manifested toward us, that God has sent His only begotten Son into the world, that we might live through Him." (1 John 4:7-10)

God reveals Himself to us through His love, which is personified in Jesus. Along with the challenge to abide in God is the calling to dwell in God's presence. In some ways, the idea of dwelling in one place is similar to the concept of abiding. According to Webster's dictionary, to "dwell" is to "live or stay as a permanent resident" and "to live or continue in a given condition or state."

To dwell in God's presence is to maintain a constant awareness of the divine in your everyday life. You put your complete trust in God and rely on His protection, help, and guidance. As you face life's challenges, you are unfazed because you recognize the nearness of God's presence.

This is an instant game-changer. Many people let their struggles, uncertainties, or worries hold them back from reaching their full potential. They wander from place to place, from job to job, and from relationship to relationship. They are searching for something they can't quite find. They long for true happiness and peace, but they always feel unsatisfied.

The answer to this problem is simple. When we choose to make God our dwelling place, regardless of our circumstances, we experience a newfound sense of joy and contentment that isn't available elsewhere. Everything changes when we choose to seek God daily, talk with Him often, and worship Him with our thoughts and actions.

Dwelling with God will require you to set aside some time in your day. In our busy world, this can be quite a challenge. However, it's also an incredible act of trust to pause and recognize that God is in control (and we are not). Let's give it a try right now. Pause for one moment and picture yourself with God. Imagine that you're sitting across from each other face-to-face as you would with a friend in a coffee shop or your significant other in your favorite restaurant. Consider what it would be like to listen to His voice and ask Him questions. Picture yourself completely wrapped up in God's presence. Block out distractions. Be quiet. Remain still. This isn't a means to some sort of end - the experience itself is the greatest reward. Simply sit, dwell, and know that God is near.

Abide in Action: The Author of Life

We were thrilled to have the young missionary couple visiting our church. They had been faithful to God's calling in their life, and God had blessed them.

However, they felt one thing was missing. This couple desperately wanted a child, but after trying for years, they were unable to conceive. Sensing that God might be ready to move in their lives, I invited them forward so we could pray over them.

As I prayed on their behalf, I laid my hands on their shoulders. My wife placed her hand on the woman's stomach, and I spoke the words I felt God had put on my heart at that moment:

"You are having a baby!"

Obviously, those are easy words to say. They heard those same words many times previously before ultimately being disappointed that it didn't come to pass. Still, something about this day felt different.

A couple of months went by before we received word that they were expecting. They soon welcomed their first little girl and added a second girl a few years later. Somehow, they were able to have two beautiful daughters after struggling to conceive for several years.

Some people will call it circumstance, but we know the truth. God works in mighty ways when we, as His followers, make the decision to abide in His goodness and provision. Throughout the years of failing to conceive, this couple never lost hope that God was sovereign. Their patience was rewarded, and we were overjoyed to celebrate with them.

Chapter Five: E - Everything

Throughout His ministry, Jesus was highly invitational and highly challenging. Jesus was radically inclusive and welcoming, but He was also clear to each person who considered following Him that discipleship didn't come without a cost. There's no way around it – Jesus wants followers who are fully committed.

In my opinion, Christianity is not something we do. It's our identity. It's who we are. As Paul writes in Romans 1, we must not be ashamed of the Gospel of Jesus Christ because it is God's power to bring salvation to all who believe. Once we experience this radical life change and transformation, it's impossible to give anything less than our best to God's mission.

In one particular example from Scripture, Jesus notices a large group following Him after witnessing one of His miracles. They want to know more about Jesus and His ministry, but when they learn more about the cost of discipleship, they change their minds and decide not to follow Him (John 6:60-66).

In another situation, Jesus illustrates the cost of discipleship with the same cross that He would eventually take up Himself. In Luke 9:23, Jesus says to anyone who will listen, "If anyone desires to come after Me, let him deny himself, and take up his cross daily, and follow Me."

These are hard teachings to hear, but the message is not difficult to understand. Anyone who desires to follow Jesus must be willing to sacrifice everything. By being willing to fully submit yourself, you will see how God's power can impact each area of your life. You'll discover a new purpose in both the blessings and the struggles. You will look at your circumstances not through a worldly lens, but you will begin to see things as God sees them.

Giving everything over to God requires us to seek first the kingdom above all else. When we do this, God will meet all of our physical and psychological needs. He will become our deepest source of joy, peace, and contentment. You will abide in Christ by loving, serving, trusting, and seeking Him before anyone or anything else.

This is the new life that God has called us to live. In Romans 8, Paul reminds us that there is no condemnation for those in Christ Jesus (Romans 8:1). Because of Jesus' death on the cross, we experience salvation from our sins and the freedom to live a new life in Christ. This new birth requires a transformation of our hearts and minds to look more like Christ's (see Romans 12:1-3 or 2 Corinthians 5:17).

While this may sound too good to be true for some, I've seen it happen time and time again for people who are willing to put the ABIDE principles into practice in their life. Doing so will require you to deny yourself and exalt Christ above anyone or anything else. It's not easy, but it is the most worthwhile initiative you will ever take.

Part Two
Bearing Fruit

If you can't already tell, I'm a huge fan of The Abide Factor. Because it is inspired by the teachings of Jesus, I believe it includes all the components necessary to facilitate meaningful transformation and life change.

As you continue to focus on The Abide Factor, your perception of the world will change, and your actions will quickly follow suit. The purpose of the first section was to help you see yourself and your surroundings differently. The next section is all about how you apply your new understanding to your everyday life.

In John 15, Jesus tells His disciples that they will bear fruit if they decide to abide in Him. As we move into the second half of this book, we will introduce you to seven practical ways you can bear fruit as you abide in Christ. By putting these principles into practice, you'll gain a better understanding of your purpose in this world and who God created you to be.

When you adopt these concepts for yourself, you create an environment where you can grow into the person God made you to be. You'll find intense healing and invigorating restoration. You'll find relief from every wound or injury. You'll feel a greater degree of spiritual, physical, mental, and emotional health than you have ever experienced before.

As Jesus says in John 10:10, "The thief does not come except to steal, and to kill, and to destroy. I have come that they may have life, and that they may have it more abundantly." (NKJV) Although Jesus is speaking to a group in this context, His teaching also applies to each of His followers on an individual level. Jesus wants you to live abundantly, and He gives you the keys to unlock the door to a more abundant life.

You are fearfully and wonderfully made by God. As the Psalmist says in Psalm 139:14, "I will praise You, for I am fearfully and wonderfully made; Marvelous are Your works, And that my soul knows very well." You are a being with many different facets and dimensions. God made you with a specific plan and purpose in mind. There's so much inside of you that you're about to discover, and I can't wait to go with you on this journey.

This section will read a little differently than what you've read so far. In the first section, our goal was to build a foundation that would begin changing the way you think. This is why each chapter was highly content-driven. I believe this next step in the process is best learned through application, so I've created the following section to read more like a workbook. Each chapter will include powerful questions for deeper reflection as well as action steps that you can immediately implement into your daily life.

You may feel that the best way to implement these practices is to partner with an experienced mentor who can walk alongside you as you look to redesign your life around the teachings of Jesus. If that's something you're interested in, we have several mentors who would love to team up with you. Learn more about our mentorship program on our website at www.provenresultsmentors.com.

Chapter Six: Spiritual Development

What is it? Spiritual development involves aligning our hearts and minds with the values and teachings of Jesus. Practically speaking, it often means sitting still and spending time in prayer and in God's Word.

Why is it important? Our spirits are the ultimate source of our well-being. We must make every effort to protect our hearts from negative influences and stay connected to Jesus at all times.

What does it make possible in your life? When we take care of our hearts, everything else in life falls into place. We must allow the Holy Spirit to take over our hearts. Once we do, we'll experience amazing transformation and develop spiritual wisdom to help us persevere through life's most difficult challenges.

Ask: On a scale of 1-10, how would you rate your spiritual health? What could you do to raise your rating by 1-2 points in the next three months?

Seek: God's protection of your heart and mind. "Keep your heart with all diligence, For out of it spring the issues of life." - Proverbs 4:23

Do: A recent study performed by the Cleveland Clinic showed that spending a few minutes each day sitting in silence can have numerous benefits for your physical and mental health. Set aside 15 minutes each day to spend alone with God. You can spend this time reading Scripture, praying, reading a Christian book, or reflecting on God's blessing in your lives. Try to eliminate any potential distractions so that you can focus all of your attention on God's presence during this time.

Chapter Seven: Character Development

What is it? God created you with unique skills and attributes that you can use to build His kingdom and serve others. When we develop our character, we are strengthening our best attributes so we can succeed in every arena in life.

Why is it important? What you feed grows, and what you starve dies. If you commit to growing in knowledge and skills, you will create opportunities to influence others and make a positive impact in the world.

What does it make possible in your life? As our character develops, we gain a better perspective on what's truly important in life. We learn that money, power, and possessions ultimately don't fulfill us, and we pursue traits and qualities that offer greater eternal value.

Ask: What's the best aspect of your character? What's one area you could improve or develop?

Seek: God's power to transform your heart and mind. "And do not be conformed to this world, but be transformed by the renewing of your mind, that you may prove what is that good and acceptable and perfect will of God." (Romans 12:2 NKJV)

Do: A study performed by The Progression Playbook reveals that reading for 15 minutes a day will deepen your knowledge and increase your capacity for empathy. Choose a book to read for 15 minutes each day. Try to find a book that covers a skill you want to develop or a topic you would like to learn more about.

Chapter Eight: Significant Relationships

What is it? Relationships, not tasks, are what make life worth living. It's easy to focus on a to-do list without setting aside enough time to spend with the important people in your life.

Why is it important? Your relationships are like your bank account. If you never make deposits, you'll eventually deplete the account. Think about how you can invest in your key relationships on a regular basis so they continue to deepen and grow.

What does it make possible in your life? Physical face-to-face time with loved ones is connected with a reduced risk of depression, anxiety, and mental illness. You'll also develop a stronger network of emotional support that can help you withstand life's challenges.

Ask: What are the 2-3 most important relationships in your life after your relationship with God? What are you doing to invest in these relationships?

Seek: Aim to love others as God has loved you. "Let this mind be in you which was also in Christ Jesus, who, being in the form of God, did not consider it robbery to be equal with God, but made Himself of no reputation, taking the form of a bondservant, and coming in the likeness of men." - Philippians 2:5-7

Do: Spend time daily connecting with family and friends. Show a genuine interest in them. Ask how their day went. Tell them you love them (and look for ways to show them you love them).

Chapter Nine: Spending/Financial

What is it? If you don't control your money, you allow your money to control you. We must develop financial discipline so that we can be sure that we are serving God and not money. One example of financial discipline we see throughout Scripture is a tithe, or giving 10% of our gross income back to God (see Abraham's tithe in Genesis 14:20).

Why is it important? If we aren't careful, we'll start to believe that money is what brings us peace. God blesses us in abundance, and He blesses us when we are in need. We must rely on God – not money – to meet our physical and spiritual needs.

What does it make possible in your life? When you put your faith in God and not money, you unlock a new realm of joy and peace that is unlike anything you've experienced before. You learn the same "secret to contentment" that Paul speaks about in Philippians 4 when he says that he can thrive in any situation when he relies on Christ's strength.

Ask: If a stranger looked at your credit card statement or monthly budget, what would they learn about your priorities and your values?

Seek: Prioritize the pursuit of righteousness above all else. ""Therefore do not worry, saying, 'What shall we eat?' or 'What shall we drink?' or 'What shall we wear?' For after all these things the Gentiles seek. For your heavenly Father knows that you need all these things. But seek first the kingdom of God and His righteousness, and all these things shall be added to you." - Matthew 6:31-33

Do: Make a financial sacrifice this week. For example, drink coffee at home instead of buying a cup from a coffee shop. See how God leads you to use the money and pay attention to what happens inside of you as you change your actions.

Chapter Ten: Rhythm of Rest

What is it? When we practice rest, we are expressing a greater level of trust in God. We are telling God that we rely on His power (and not our own effort) to keep our lives in motion.

Why is it important? God Himself set an example for us to follow by resting on the seventh day after finishing creation (Genesis 2:2-3). If you never set aside time to rest, your body and mind will quickly break down. We must recognize our own humanity and our inability to stay constantly in motion.

What does it make possible in your life? Setting aside time to rest is a difficult discipline to develop in today's world. However, you will be far more energized and productive if you give your body and mind an occasional break.

Ask: How do you incorporate rest into your daily, weekly, and seasonal rhythms? How could you improve the quality of your rest?

Seek: Pursue the peace that comes from knowing God is in control. "Come to Me, all you who labor and are heavy laden, and I will give you rest. Take My yoke upon you and learn from Me, for I am gentle and lowly in heart, and you will find rest for your souls. For My yoke is easy and My burden is light." - Matthew 11:28-30

Do: Make a point of getting at least seven hours of sleep each night. Go to bed earlier if needed. Prepare yourself for bed by putting away your phone and getting off social media about an hour before you fall asleep.

Chapter Eleven: Daily Priority

What is it? If everything is important, nothing is important. Many of us waste time on tasks that don't get us closer to our desired goals. The enemy tries to steal our focus by distracting us, so we must determine what our priorities are.

Why is it important? Everyone multi-tasks, but nobody can multi-focus. For example, you may try to have a conversation with a friend while responding to a text message on your phone, but you can't physically focus on both tasks at the same time. Your brain will quickly grow tired, and you'll feel mental fog setting in.

What does it make possible in your life? When we learn how to prioritize our tasks each day, we will reduce our stress and have a clear sense of our purpose and direction.

Ask: If you could only accomplish 2-3 things on a given day, what would those tasks be? What makes them important?

Seek: Consider what priorities God wants you to focus on. Reflect on Jesus' words to Martha in Luke 10: "And Jesus answered and said to her, "Martha, Martha, you are worried and troubled about many things. But one thing is needed, and Mary has chosen that good part, which will not be taken away from her." (Luke 10:41-42 NKJV)

Do: Eliminate any commitments or habits that drain your focus or energy from what truly matters. Spend less time watching TV or flipping through social media. Use the extra time to work on your most important tasks.

Chapter Twelve: Physical

What is it? In 1 Timothy 4, Paul tells Timothy that physical training has "some" value. He goes on to say that godliness has greater value, but he still hints at the importance of maintaining your physical health. Our bodies are temples of the Holy Spirit, and we should make our physical health a priority.

Why is it important? The physical, mental, and emotional benefits of improved health are numerous. You'll have more energy and less brain fog. You'll limit aches and pains. You'll naturally reduce depression and anxiety, and you'll lower your blood pressure levels. These are just a few examples of the positive impact that physical health can have.

What does it make possible in your life? When we take care of our bodies, we're able to live life without restrictions. We can serve Jesus, enjoy our family, connect with friends, make a meaningful impact through our work, and participate in hobbies without physical limitations holding us back.

Ask: Imagine that you're in the best shape of your life. How would that improve your current situation?

Seek: Gratitude for whatever level of health you have. If you're in good physical condition, thank God for His blessing on your life. If you're suffering from a long-term illness or disease, trust God for strength and healing.

Do: Commit to some level of physical activity. This doesn't mean you have to run a marathon or take up CrossFit. Perhaps for you, physical activity looks like taking a walk with your spouse or setting up a pick-up basketball game with some friends. The specific activity doesn't matter as much as making the decision to do something.

Conclusion and Next Steps

We've reached the end of one journey and the beginning of another. By now, you understand The Abide Factor in detail. You know how to pursue and adopt the calling God has placed on your life. You've seen numerous true accounts of what God's power makes possible on this side of Heaven. So what will you do now?

I'd like to leave you with one important truth before we wrap up. Throughout this book, I've shared plenty of stories from my 37-plus years in ministry. I have many other stories I would like to tell you, but I'll save those for the next book (or perhaps a conversation over lunch or a cup of coffee). Time and time again, I've seen God's hand at work in the world. At the same time, there are many things we've prayed for or believed that God would do that we haven't yet seen happen.

This doesn't weaken my faith because I believe in God's timing and not my own. Furthermore, there's a tremendous opportunity for each of us to learn and grow as we wait for God to act. I see many people miss out on what God has in store for them because they are unwilling (or unable) to wait. When times get hard, many people walk away and look for another answer.

If you're going to learn to abide in Christ, you must know how to wait well. Here are four practical ways that you can remain obedient to God while waiting:

- **Stay faithful.** "Being confident of this very thing, that He which hath begun a good work in you will perform it until the day of Jesus Christ." - Philippians 1:6
- **Remain patient.** "Therefore be patient, brethren, until the coming of the Lord. See how the farmer waits for the precious fruit of the earth, waiting patiently for it until it receives the early and latter rain. You also be patient. Establish your hearts, for the coming of the Lord is at hand." - James 5:7-8
- **Trust.** "Trust in the Lord with all your heart, and lean not on your own understanding; in all your ways acknowledge Him, and He shall direct your paths." - Proverbs 3:5-6
- **Wait on the Lord.** "Wait on the Lord; be of good courage, and He shall strengthen your heart; wait, I say, on the Lord!" - Psalm 27:14
- **They say good things come to those who wait.** I believe better things come to those who trust in God and abide in Christ while they wait.
- **I love you, and God loves you.** You are in my prayers as you put the principles from this book into practice.

Afterword

There's a common saying that you become like the five people who you spend the most time with. It's easy to see why this would happen. As human beings, we are social creatures. We crave acceptance and long to belong to a community or tribe.

You'll likely struggle to reach your potential when you surround yourself with the wrong people. For example, if you want to get in better shape but you spend time with friends who aren't physically active, you'll likely fail to make progress. If you want to succeed in your career, but you surround yourself with people who are apathetic about their work, you probably won't receive the encouragement or support you need to move forward.

At the same time, you can increase your chances of success by strategically choosing the people in your inner circle. As we read in Proverbs 17, "As iron sharpens iron, So a man sharpens the countenance of his friend." Surround yourself with people who sharpen you, encourage you, challenge you, and push you to become the best version of yourself.

We want to help you make this happen. If you would like to participate in a godly, life-giving community that will walk alongside you as you seek to apply these teachings, I hope you'll reach out to us directly. Our passion is to create mentoring relationships that help men and women transform into the image of Christ by applying these teachings. We would love to walk alongside you as you grow in your faith and obedience to Christ. You can learn more about our mentorship program on our website at www.provenresultsmentors.com.

About the Author

Shawn Lyons

Pastor Shawn Lyons was called to ministry 48 years ago as a 12-year-old boy. He serves at the Harvest Church in Derry, PA, where his ministry has reached over 95 countries and 48 of the 50 US states. He is passionate about preaching and teaching the Word of God and serving in the church alongside his wife, Susan.

Pastor Shawn is excited to share the powerful message of "The Abide Factor" in his new book. He's been married to his incredible wife, Susan, for 38 years. Together, they have three children and two grandsons. When he's not serving in the church or spending time with his family, he enjoys golfing.